FREAKY FREELOADERS

BUGS THAT FEED ON PEOPLE

MITES

LORRAINE HARRISON

PowerKiDS press

New York

Published in 2016 by The Rosen Publishing Group, Inc.
29 East 21st Street, New York, NY 10010

First Edition

Editor: Katie Kawa
Book Design: Michael J. Flynn

Photo Credits: Cover, pp. 1, 16 Steve Gschmeissner/Science Photo Library/Getty Images; cover, pp. 3–24 (frame) Dinga/Shutterstock.com; pp. 4, 6, 10, 12, 18, 20 (mite) 3drenderings/Shutterstock.com; p. 5 Science Picture Co/Collection Mix: Subjects/Getty Images; p. 7 Juan Gaertner/Shutterstock.com; p. 8 Agency-Animal-Picture/Getty Images; p. 9 Heiko Kiera/Shutterstock.com; p. 11 BSIP/Universal Images Group/Getty Images; p. 13 http://upload.wikimedia.org/wikipedia/commons/2/21/Chigger_bites.jpg; p. 14 molekuul.be/Shutterstock.com; p. 15 SCIEPRO/Science Photo Library/Getty Images; p. 19 Michael Wunderli/www.flickr.com/photos/56006259@N06/14399018671/CC BY-SA 2.0; p. 21 bmf-foto.de/Shutterstock.com; p. 22 Marcel Jancovic/Shutterstock.com.

Library of Congress Cataloging-in-Publication Data

Harrison, Lorraine, author.
 Mites / Lorraine Harrison.
   pages cm. — (Freaky freeloaders: Bugs that feed on people)
 Includes bibliographical references and index.
 ISBN 978-1-4994-0759-4 (pbk.)
 ISBN 978-1-4994-0760-0 (6 pack)
 ISBN 978-1-4994-0761-7 (library binding)
 1. Mites—Juvenile literature. I. Title. II. Series: Freaky freeloaders. Bugs that feed on people.
 QL458.H38 2015
 595.4'2—dc23
                          2015008573

Manufactured in the United States of America

CPSIA Compliance Information: Batch #WS15PK: For Further Information contact Rosen Publishing, New York, New York at 1-800-237-9932

CONTENTS

MITE-Y PARASITES

Mites are tiny animals that sometimes cause big problems for people. These creepy creatures are between 0.004 inch and 0.25 inch (0.1 mm and 6 mm) long. They have eight legs like a spider.

Some species, or kinds, of mites are parasites. Parasites are animals that feed on the bodies of other animals, which are called hosts. Mites that are parasites live on many different hosts. Most mites don't bother people, but some bite people to feed on their blood.

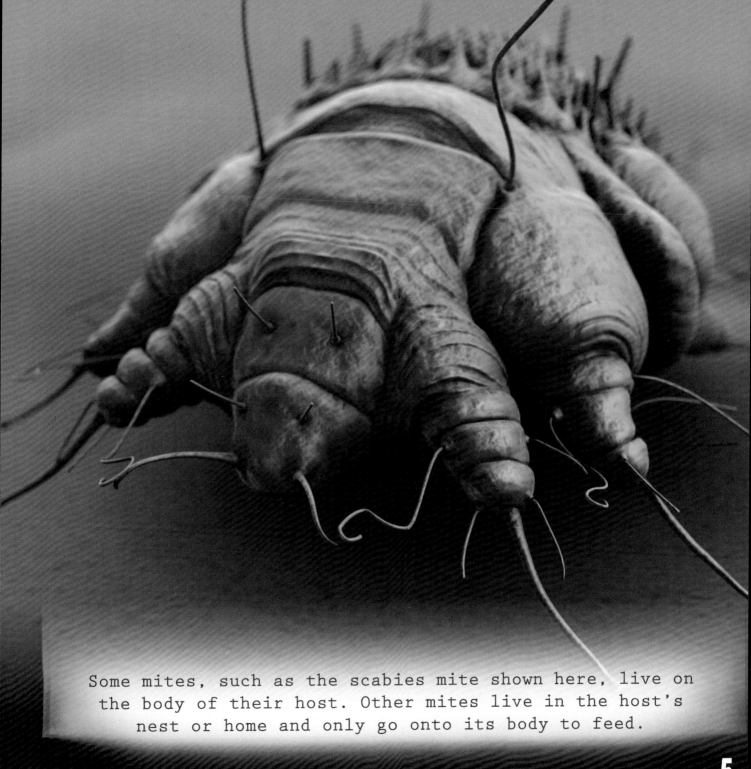

Some mites, such as the scabies mite shown here, live on the body of their host. Other mites live in the host's nest or home and only go onto its body to feed.

THOUSANDS OF SPECIES

Mites live all over the world—from the bodies of animals to the soil. **Scientists** believe there are over 45,000 species of mites alive today. Very few of these thousands of species live on people.

Some mites are actually helpful. They live on tree trunks and other plants, and they break down the bodies of dead plants and animals to make the soil richer. Other mites live on animals such as dogs and rats, but could bite people if they're the only hosts around.

FREAKY FACT!

SCIENTISTS BELIEVE MITES LIVED ON
EARTH AS FAR BACK AS 230 MILLION
YEARS AGO.

Dust mites, shown here, don't feed on people's bodies, but some people are **allergic** to them. These mites can cause people to sneeze!

RAT MITES AND BIRD MITES

Some of the most common mites people find in their home and on their body are mites that usually feed on other animals. The rat mite commonly feeds on the blood of rats, as its name suggests. However, if there are no longer any rats present in an area, these mites will move to people's bodies instead.

Bird mites, such as the chicken mite, move from birds to people for food if birds are nowhere to be found.

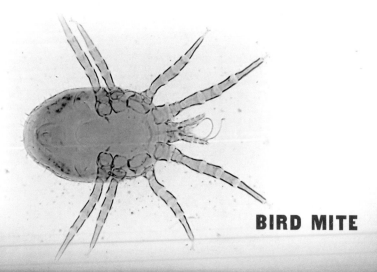

BIRD MITE

Rat mites are one of the most common species of mites
found in people's homes. They're commonly found after a
large group of rats are taken out of an area.

A MITE'S LIFE CYCLE

All mites share the same basic **life cycle**. They start their lives as eggs laid by an adult female. Then, they grow into larvae. You can tell a mite larva from an adult mite by counting its legs. A mite larva only has six legs. Next, mites enter the nymph **stage**, and then they become adults.

Certain mite species only feed on blood when they're larvae. These mite larvae are called chiggers, and they've been known to bite people.

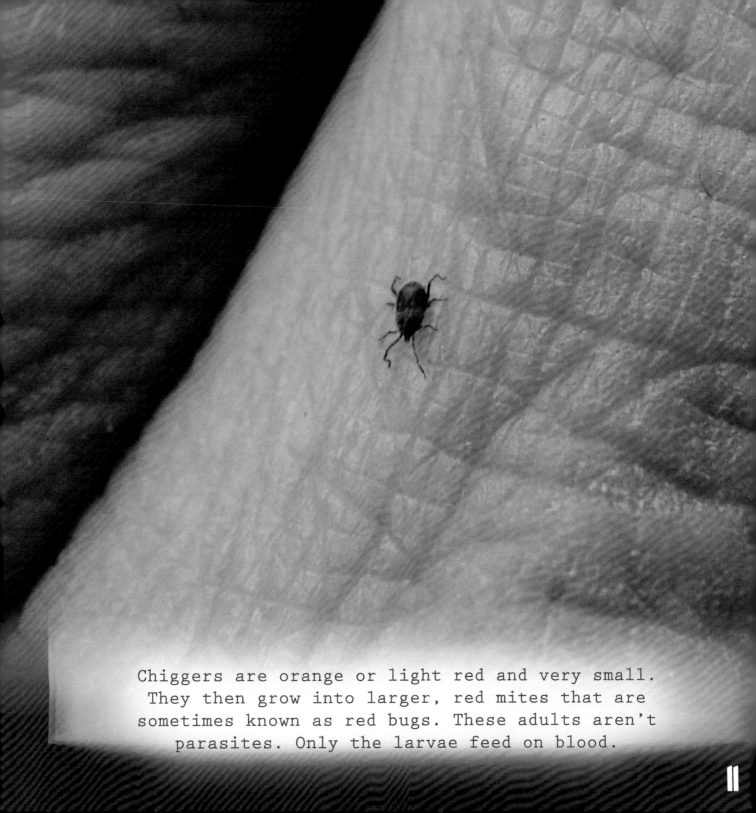

Chiggers are orange or light red and very small. They then grow into larger, red mites that are sometimes known as red bugs. These adults aren't parasites. Only the larvae feed on blood.

LOOK OUT FOR CHIGGERS!

Most mites that live on humans burrow, or dig, into the skin of their host. A chigger, however, stays on the host's skin and **injects** a **liquid** into the skin that makes a hard area around the parasite.

Chigger bites appear as red, raised areas on the skin. These areas are very **itchy**. Chigger bites are most often found in places on the body where clothing fits tightly against the skin. These places include the ankles, around the waist, and under the arms.

FREAKY FACT!

CERTAIN PARASITES CAN MAKE PEOPLE SICK, BUT NORTH AMERICAN CHIGGERS DON'T SPREAD SICKNESSES TO PEOPLE WHEN THEY BITE.

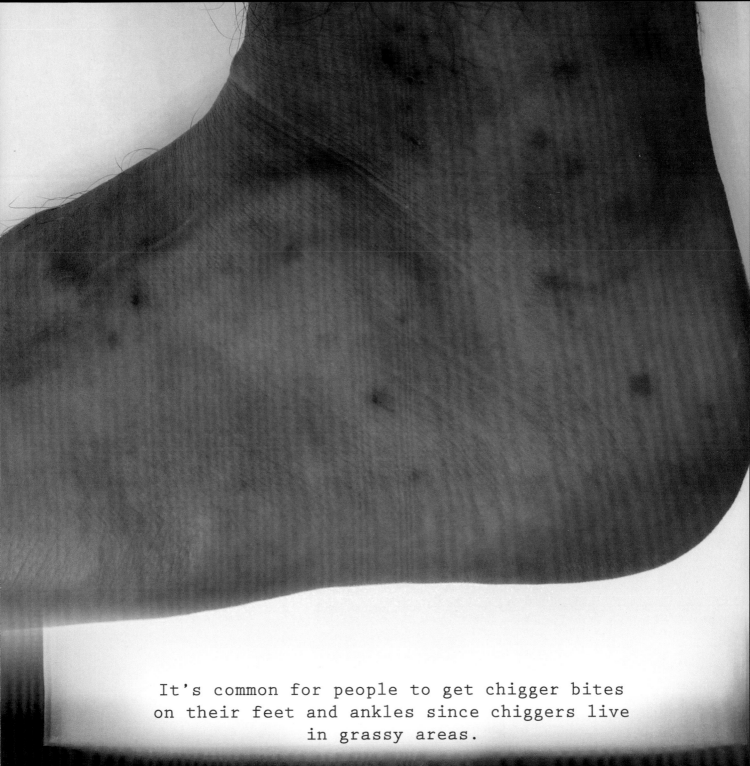

It's common for people to get chigger bites
on their feet and ankles since chiggers live
in grassy areas.

THE SCARY SCABIES MITE

Scabies mites are another group of mites that feed on people. The human scabies mite, which is also known as the human itch mite, burrows into a person's skin and causes an itchy skin problem commonly known as scabies.

Scabies mites don't feed on blood. Instead, they feed on liquids from the cells of the their hosts. They also eat dead skin cells. Scabies mites live in the upper **layer** of the skin, so they always have dead skin cells to eat.

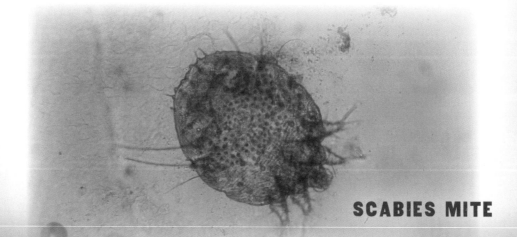

SCABIES MITE

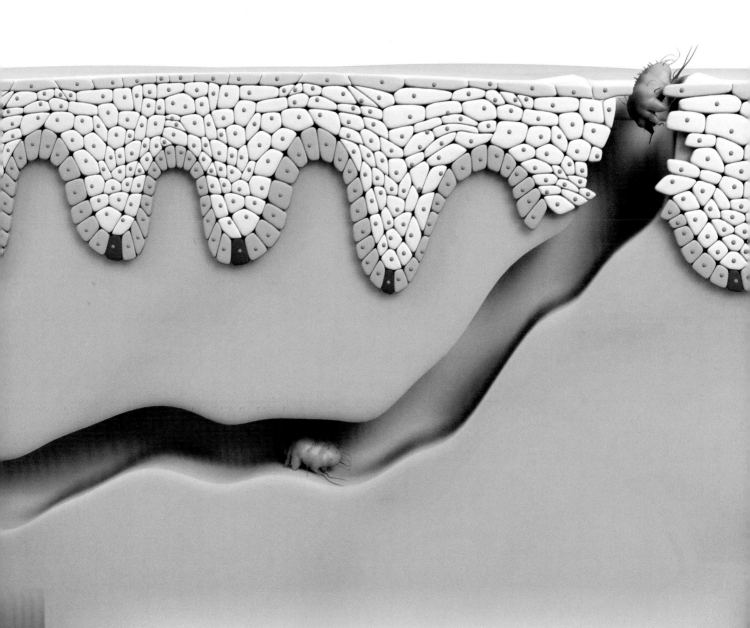

People with scabies mites don't feel itchy as soon as the mites burrow into their skin. It can take over a month before the itching starts.

GETTING UNDER YOUR SKIN

Scabies mites die if they aren't on the body of their human host. Their entire life cycle takes place on and under a person's skin.

An adult female scabies mite lays eggs as it burrows into a person's skin. When the larvae come out of the eggs, they move to the top layer of the skin and then make their own burrows. After their time as larvae, they become nymphs, which look like smaller adult scabies mites.

SCABIES MITE EGGS

Male and female scabies mites **mate** only one time in their life. From then on, the female lays eggs every day.

EGG

- small ovals
- laid under the skin of the host

LARVA

- comes out of egg after 3–5 days
- 6 legs
- creates its own molting pouch in host's skin

ADULT

- female comes out of molting pouch to find a place to lay eggs
- female lays 2–3 eggs every day for the rest of its life
- lives for 1–2 months on host's body

NYMPH

- 8 legs
- molts as it grows into an adult

FREAKY FACT!

THE SHORT BURROWS THAT SCABIES MITE LARVAE AND NYMPHS MAKE ARE CALLED MOLTING POUCHES. WHEN AN ANIMAL, SUCH AS A MITE, MOLTS, IT SHEDS ITS SKIN. MITES NEED TO MOLT IN ORDER TO BECOME ADULTS.

AN ITCHY PROBLEM

Scabies mites' burrows appear on the skin as small, crooked lines. These lines are one sign that a person has scabies. Another sign is an itchy **rash**. Scabies mites are spread from person to person by direct **contact**. These parasites can spread very quickly in close quarters.

Scabies mites are most commonly found on people's wrists, elbows, feet, and the areas between their fingers. Scabies is commonly treated by a skin doctor, or dermatologist, with special medicine.

FREAKY FACT!

SCABIES MITES CAN SPREAD FROM ONE PERSON IN A FAMILY TO THE REST OF THE FAMILY BEFORE ANY SIGNS OF SCABIES APPEAR. IF ONE FAMILY MEMBER HAS SCABIES, THE REST OF THE FAMILY SHOULD BE CHECKED FOR IT, TOO.

Shown here is what the burrow of a scabies mite looks like under a microscope, which is a tool used to make small things appear larger.

MITE CONTROL

If you think you've become a host for mites, it's important to figure out what kind of mite is living on your skin. Different mites call for different kinds of treatment and different ways to get rid of them.

For example, scabies mites can't live in high heat. If these mites are living in your skin, you should wash your clothing and bedding in hot water and then put them in the dryer. You should also see a dermatologist as soon as possible.

FREAKY FACT!

TO GET RID OF CHIGGERS ON YOUR BODY OR YOUR CLOTHES, USE WARM, SOAPY WATER.

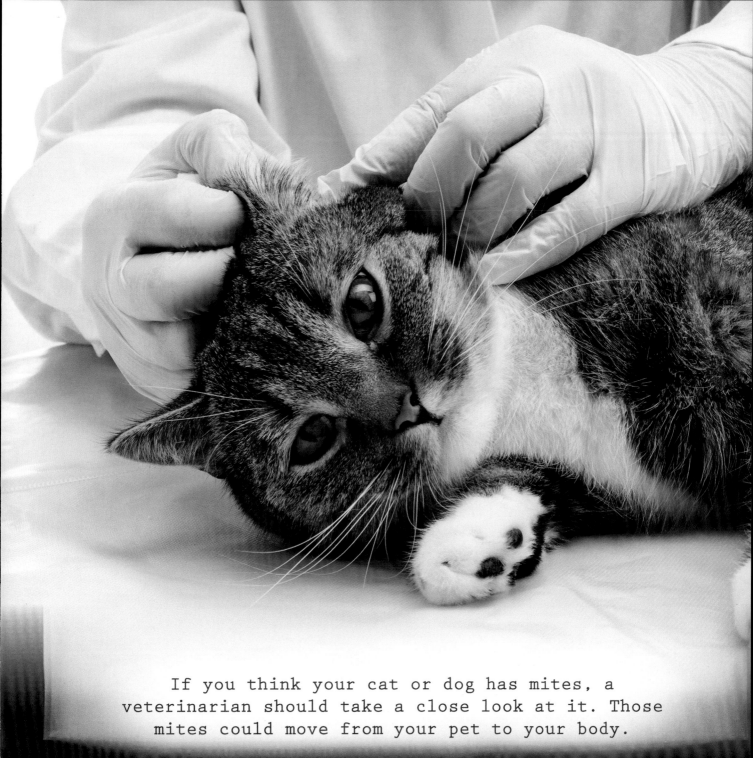

If you think your cat or dog has mites, a veterinarian should take a close look at it. Those mites could move from your pet to your body.

A MITE'S MEAL

It's weird to think of your body as food for tiny bugs, but mites can make a meal out of your skin and blood. Mites make their home on many different living things. Some mites are tiny enough to live on the bodies of bees!

Thankfully, mites don't cause people much harm, but they can make people very itchy. It's important to get rid of these parasites quickly once you spot them on your pet or on your body.

BEE MITES

allergic: Having a medical condition that causes someone to become sick after coming into contact with something that is harmless to most people.

contact: A state of touching.

inject: To put into something forcefully.

itchy: Producing an unpleasant feeling on your skin that makes you want to scratch.

layer: One thickness lying over or under another.

life cycle: The steps that a living thing goes through as it grows and dies.

liquid: Something that flows freely like water.

mate: To come together to make babies.

rash: A group of red spots on the skin.

scientist: Someone who studies the way things work and the way things are.

stage: A step in the growth of a living thing.

WEBSITES

Due to the changing nature of Internet links, PowerKids Press has developed an online list of websites related to the subject of this book. This site is updated regularly. Please use this link to access the list: www.powerkidslinks.com/bfp/mite